Executive Functioning Workbook for Kids

EXECUTIVE FUNCTIONING

WORKBOOK for KIDS

40 Fun Activities to Build Memory, Flexible Thinking, and Self-Control Skills at Home, in School, and Beyond

SHARON GRAND, PhD, BCN

CALLISTO PUBLISHING

Copyright © 2021 by Callisto Publishing LLC
Cover and internal design © 2021 by Callisto Publishing LLC
Illustrations © 2021 Collaborate Agency
Art Director: Scott Petrower
Art Producer: Hannah Dickerson
Editor: Eliza Kirby
Production Manager: Jose Olivera

Callisto Publishing and the colophon are registered trademarks of Callisto Publishing LLC

Published by Callisto Publishing LLC C/O Sourcebooks LLC
P.O. Box 4410, Naperville, Illinois 60567-4410
(630) 961-3900
callistopublishing.com

This product conforms to all applicable CPSC and CPSIA standards.

Source of Production: Wing King Tong Paper Products Co.Ltd. Shenzhen, Guangdong Province, China
Date of Production: December 2023
Run Number: 5037110

Printed and bound in China.
WKT 15

This book is dedicated
to Josh, all who have struggled
with executive functioning,
and all those who love us
and understand.

Contents

A Letter to Kids

. . . .

Welcome to this workbook!

This is a special workbook because it is all about *you*. Do you ever find yourself getting distracted? Do you have a lot of half-finished projects lying around? Do you find that you often forget things, like bringing your homework or lunch to school? Are you always looking for items like your shoes or pencils? If the answer to any of these questions is yes, then you are in the right place.

Your brain needs to do a lot of different things every day. Executive functioning skills can help you. Imagine your brain is like an orchestra. Each of the instruments plays a different sound, and they all must work together to make music. If your brain is the orchestra, then your executive functioning skills are the conductor. These skills help your brain do everything it needs to do—like focus, organize, and remember—at the appropriate times.

This book is going to show you some ways to build your executive functioning skills. It will also help you figure out which skills come more naturally to you and where you might need a little more help. In the same way that each instrument brings a different sound to the orchestra, different types of executive functioning help with different situations, such as doing homework, studying, playing sports, or completing a chore. This book will help you build and improve your skills in lots of different situations—at home, in school, and out in the world. Most important, this book will give you some tools that work like superpower gadgets: They will help you take charge of your life so you can have more time and energy to do the things you love.

A Letter to Grown-Ups

. . . .

Welcome parents, guardians, teachers, and other grown-ups

who are interested and invested in helping your child with executive functioning. If you have an intelligent, awesome kid who is struggling with being disorganized, overemotional, forgetful, or unfocused, this book is for you. Executive functioning skills comprise a unique set of skills that encompass these abilities and more. As someone who grew up with, and then raised a child with, executive functioning shortcomings, I am keenly aware of the energy it takes to function in the world when our executive functioning skills are weak and of the toll it can take on our self-esteem. What a relief it was as an adult to begin to understand what was happening. If your child is still young, I congratulate you for getting a head start on helping them understand and build these important skills.

This book is designed to help kids and parents learn together as they strengthen the "behind-the-scenes" skills that are essential for success. The book addresses the major skills that all kids need to be successful at school, at home, and out in the world. As you read, you and your child will discover 40 exercises and games that use evidence-based methods to help your child build and improve their memory, time management, focus, self-control, organization, and many other executive functioning skills. The exercises are a mix of fun activities and useful real-life tools, such as checklists and calendars. The text and explanations throughout the book are designed to help your child understand executive functioning skills, validate your child's experiences, create understanding, improve communication, and build self-esteem.

This book is not meant to be simply given to the child, but to be experienced together. I strongly encourage you to read along and work through these exercises with your child. Before you get started, take some time to read Positive Parenting and Executive Functioning Skills on page 99. It offers general guidance on helping a child who struggles with executive functioning, such as ways to frame feedback positively, that will help your child succeed.

Executive functioning challenges are expressed not only as difficulties with knowing what to do but also as difficulties with doing what you know. Learning the tools is the first part of the process. Most children will need weeks or even months of consistent practice, along with help and support from their parents, for their skills to feel natural and automatic. Complex integrative skills, such as filling in a calendar or finishing homework independently, may not be achieved for some children until middle school or beyond, and even then, only with daily routine and practice. This book provides ideas on how to improve these skills. The hard work and practice are up to you and your child. Therefore, it is important for you to engage in self-care and get support of your own.

Not every child with executive functioning challenges is the same. Other conditions, such as severe anxiety, lack of sleep, or an auditory processing disorder, may mimic executive functioning difficulties. If you are wondering whether your child has any of these conditions, a complete assessment is highly recommended. I've provided additional assessment resources (page 101), and a description of what types of professionals you might contact for an assessment or extra support (page 104).

CHAPTER 1

What Is Executive Functioning?

Have you ever wondered what it takes to be a superhero? Superheroes are smart, they do the right thing, and they are ready for anything. This is because they have three important skills. First, they have a great working memory, which means they can pay attention to clues and remember them later. Second, they have excellent self-control, which lets them take their time and make a plan before they act. Finally, they have something called mental flexibility. Mental flexibility means thinking about the same thing in lots of different ways, like we do when we are trying to figure out the answer to a puzzle or put clues together to solve a mystery. These three skills—working memory, self-control, and mental flexibility—are examples of executive functioning skills, and they help superheroes save the day.

Executive functioning skills are the part of the brain that helps people do important work. Kids need executive functioning skills, too. Working memory helps you remember to bring your homework to school, and it ensures that you don't lose things like your sneakers or pencils. Self-control helps you cooperate, be a team player, and listen to other people. Mental flexibility powers up your ability to make new plans or problem solve without getting upset about it. With these skills, it's easy to have a successful day.

How are your executive functioning skills? If you find that you often lose things, forget stuff you need, have a hard time paying attention, or have trouble changing course, that's okay. You are not alone. The good news is that you can get better at it. In fact, have you ever noticed that some superheroes have lots of gadgets that help them do their jobs? From boots that help them climb buildings to pens that write in invisible ink, it's easier to be a superhero when you have a bunch of cool stuff to help you. The executive functioning skill tools that you'll learn from this book are a lot like the gadgets used by superheroes: They help everyday kids do the super things they want to do every day.

SUPERHERO SIDEKICKS

Superheroes often have challenges that they can't solve by themselves. This is why they have sidekicks to help them. Their sidekicks might fight alongside them, create a gadget, or help find a solution. Kids can have sidekicks, too. They may be parents, teachers, coaches, or other trusted adults.

Start by explaining one of your challenges to a sidekick. Describe a time when you experienced a challenge with executive functioning skills. This may be a time when it was challenging for you to listen, remember, think before acting, or change course. (For instance, maybe you had a hard time stopping a behavior, changing a belief, or moving from one task to another.)

....

....

....

....

....

....

....

....

....

....

....

....

EMOTION SEARCH

We all want to be successful, and it isn't easy when we are challenged. What kinds of emotions did you feel when you had the experience you wrote about in Exercise 1? Find those emotions in the list below and circle each one you felt. Difficult feelings like these are clues that it's time to problem solve and ask for help. What kinds of feelings do you think a superhero has when they are not successful right away? Look for those feelings in the list below and circle them using a different color. Are there some feelings you and your imagined superhero have in common?

Angry	**Grumpy**
Anxious	**Guilty**
Determined	**Sad**
Disappointed	**Stressed**
Embarrassed	**Upset**
Frustrated	**Worried**

How do you feel when you *are* successful?

....

DO I *REALLY* NEED THESE SKILLS?

Yes! Having great executive functioning skills can help you be more successful every day. For example, Deshawn and Charlie are friends in the second grade. Deshawn has a great working memory. He gets up in the morning, finds everything he needs, and goes to school on time. Charlie gets up in the morning, can't find his homework, and is missing a shoe, which makes him late for school. Deshawn also has great self-control. He sits quietly and follows his teacher's instructions. Charlie gets in trouble for talking too much and has a hard time getting started on the assignments. While Charlie is struggling, Deshawn's executive functioning skills are helping him get through the day.

Now let's talk about two other friends, Samira and Skylar, who are on a soccer team together. Samira's working memory helps her brings her equipment bag to practice. Skylar forgot to put her shin guards in her bag, so she has to wait for her dad to bring them to the field before she can begin to play. Samira has great mental flexibility and self-control, and so she knows when to try for a goal and when to pass the ball to other players. Skylar has a harder time with these skills, so she tends to hog the ball. Having great executive functioning skills helps Samira be a team player, just like it helps Deshawn do well in school. Even grown-ups need executive functioning skills to stay organized, take care of the house, or plan a great vacation. Executive functioning skills help us succeed, be confident, and feel great about ourselves.

WORKING MEMORY CLUE CARDS

Clue cards are cards that you can attach to your backpack, sports bag, or a wall in your home. These cards help you remember everything you need by giving you a short list you can follow. Look at the Morning Checklist example below, then write your own clue cards. You can use note cards or cardboard or even get your cards laminated.

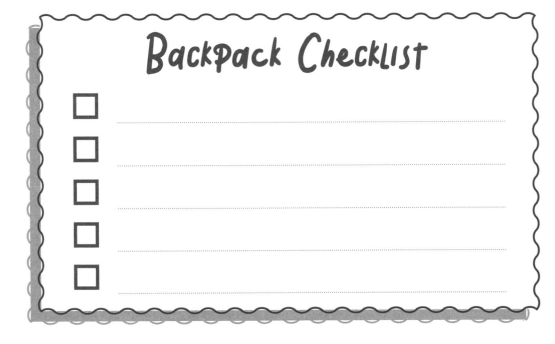

Morning Checklist

- ☐ Brush teeth
- ☐ Wash face
- ☐ Have breakfast
- ☐ Get dressed
- ☐ Check calendar

Backpack Checklist

- ☐ ....
- ☐ ....
- ☐ ....
- ☐ ....
- ☐ ....

Bedtime Checklist

- [ ]
- [ ]
- [ ]
- [ ]
- [ ]

Checklist

_____
(Activity)

- [ ]
- [ ]
- [ ]
- [ ]
- [ ]

I AM SIMON

Have you ever played Simon Says? In order to win the game, you need to have self-control to resist your impulses and only follow the directions that start with "Simon says." That means, in order to succeed, before you do anything, you have to stop and think.

You can try being Simon. Simply pause, take a breath, and replace Simon's name with your own. It's great to schedule times to play this, but you can also use it whenever necessary. Let's practice.

Before I walk into class

(Take a deep breath) .... says, "Enter quietly."

Your name

When it's not my turn

(Take a deep breath) .... says, "Wait for my turn."

Your name

Now, make up some of your own. What are some things you can say to yourself to help you get through the day? Circle the ones you want to try today:

_____ says, "I can do this."
Your name

_____ says, "Be patient."
Your name

_____ says, "Use kind words."
Your name

_____ says, "Quiet hands."
Your name

_____ says, "Try again."
Your name

What else can you say?

....

....

....

....

....

THE POWER OF POSITIVE THINKING

Changing our thoughts can change the way we feel and help us build success. One way to do this is with a growth mindset. A growth mindset views both challenges and failures as opportunities to learn and get stronger. If you don't do well on a math test, you might think, "I'm bad at math." If you think about that situation with a growth mindset, you might instead think, "I can review the test and do better next time."

Change the thoughts below into a growth mindset. Match the thoughts on the left with its growth mindset alternative on the right. You can choose more than one answer. Then come up with a few of your own.

I can't do it.	**I can learn how to do it.**
I'm not good at this.	**I will be able to do it if I keep trying.**
It's too hard.	**It will get easier with practice.**
I don't know how to do this.	**I can ask for help.**
I have to do it myself.	**I'm not good at this yet, but I will get better.**

What other thoughts can be changed to a growth mindset alternative?

Thought	Growth Mindset Alternative Thought

GETTING TO KNOW MY BRAIN

Now that you have been introduced to three of the main brain skills that are used for executive functioning, let's get to know each one a little better. Getting familiar with each skill will help us understand how all three work together.

WORKING MEMORY

When we learn something new, we rely on our working memory to keep the new information active so we can do something with it. For instance, working memory helps us remember what someone just said so we can respond to it. Working memory helps us focus, organize, and problem solve. It is important for many tasks, such as following instructions, responding in a conversation, or playing a game.

SELF-CONTROL

Self-control takes the information from working memory and helps us see what is most important. It also helps us resist impulses to do things that are not necessary or helpful. For instance, let's imagine that your mom told you she is on an important phone call. While she is on the phone, you think of something you want to tell her. Working memory helps you remember that the call is important. Self-control helps you prioritize the call as important and helps you wait and let her finish. Self-control helps us stop and think, choose the correct action, and avoid actions that are impulsive or distracting.

MENTAL FLEXIBILITY

Mental flexibility is our ability to change our thoughts or our course of action. For instance, in the scenario above, mental flexibility can help you change your thoughts from "I can't wait for Mom to get off the phone" to "I can try harder to wait." It can also help you change course of action. For example, you might decide to draw a picture or play with your sibling while you wait. Do you think it will be easier for Mom to listen to you when she is off the phone? Imagine how happy you will feel when your executive functioning skills help you wait successfully.

You are doing great! Are you ready to join the Superhero Academy? In the next chapter, you will discover 10 more skills that all superheroes need to succeed.

CHAPTER 2

Understanding Executive Functioning

10 MORE MAJOR SKILLS

Welcome to the Superhero Academy! In chapter 1, we learned about working memory, self-control, and mental flexibility. Here we will learn all about 10 more executive functioning skills and how these skills work together to make us stronger, braver, and more confident in our everyday life.

COMPLETING TASKS

Completing tasks means finishing what we have started. Most of the time, it is helpful to finish one thing before we move on to another. Completing tasks takes persistence, which means continuing to do the task even if we get bored, tired, or frustrated. It also means knowing how to get back to a task after a break.

CHOOSING GOALS AND STICKING TO THEM

This is also known as goal-oriented persistence. Perhaps you have a goal, such as getting an A on a test or making a special basketball shot. Goal-oriented persistence is determining what you have to do to complete your goal, sticking with it, and ignoring all other distractions.

STAYING FOCUSED

Staying focused is the action skill that allows you to pay attention to a task. Staying focused means avoiding distractions and keeping your effort and energy going. You can imagine your focus like a flashlight that you are holding in a dark room. Focus helps you shine your light only on what you want to pay attention to.

CONTROLLING EMOTIONS

When our emotions become too big, they can stop our executive functioning skills from working. For instance, it is hard to focus if we are upset, angry, or even excited. Emotional self-control is the skill that helps us calm our emotions so that we can manage our behaviors and thoughts.

BEING SELF-AWARE

Being self-aware is the ability to slow down and observe your thoughts, feelings, and behaviors. It also helps us become aware of our physical bodies, such as when we are feeling tired or hungry. Being self-aware helps us observe ourselves and choose actions that produce positive results.

THINKING BEFORE ACTING

Thinking before acting is also known as response inhibition. The word *inhibition* means to stop something. So, this skill is used when we want to stop an action that is inappropriate or interferes with our goals. For instance, this skill might come in handy to help you stop talking during class.

STARTING TASKS

Starting tasks is the ability to begin a task or to stop one task and start another. Almost anyone can begin a task they are excited about, but it takes a lot more energy and focus to start a task that you are less interested in. Difficulty with starting tasks can sometimes be mistaken for being lazy or uncooperative.

BEING ORGANIZED

Being organized is a skill that allows us to put things in a proper place so that they can be found and used easily and quickly. When your space is organized, it appears neat and you can always find what you're looking for in the same place. This allows us to spend less time looking for things we need.

THOUGHTFUL PLANNING

Thoughtful planning is the ability to create a road map to reach a goal. Most tasks have several steps, so it is helpful to have a plan to know what the steps are and put them in an order that makes sense. Prioritizing is a part of planning; it helps us decide what steps are most important so we can know what to focus on first.

MANAGING TIME

Managing time is a skill that helps us meet time limits or deadlines. It involves making a good guess about how long something will take and then planning your time wisely. For instance, if you need 15 minutes to get ready for baseball and you are leaving at 6:00, you should start getting ready at 5:45.

As you work through this chapter, remember that everyone has all these executive functioning skills and the power to use them. Just like any superhero, we can make our powers stronger by practicing, asking for help, getting tools we need, and never giving up. This book will help you make your skills stronger. As your skills get stronger, you succeed more, your confidence grows, and you feel great. Are you ready to move on?

BUILDING MY BRAINPOWER

To have strong executive functioning skills, we need strong brains. Our brains need water, protein, sleep, and exercise to stay strong. When we don't eat, sleep, drink water, or move our bodies, we can become tired and grumpy. Ask your sidekick (a parent, teacher, or caregiver) to help you set some goals, and then use this chart as a guide for taking care of your brain.

Name: _____   Date Started: _____

	SUN	MON	TUE	WED	THU	FRI	SAT
Ate enough protein							
Drank enough water							
Met my exercise goal							
Got enough sleep							
How do I feel today? (Circle a number)	Great 5 4 3 2 1 Poor	Great 5 4 3 2 1 Poor	Great 5 4 3 2 1 Poor	Great 5 4 3 2 1 Poor	Great 5 4 3 2 1 Poor	Great 5 4 3 2 1 Poor	Great 5 4 3 2 1 Poor

Wow! Great job! Now that you are taking such good care of your brain, how do you feel?

Happy   Calm   Excited   Rested   Awesome   Smart   Confident

GETTING TO KNOW MYSELF

Now, you superhero, let's talk about expectations. Some people think success comes easily. This is false. We all have things we are good at, like math or baseball, for instance. But no one is good at everything. Most success comes from learning, hard work, and practice.

When you are working toward success, you should expect to *learn*. We all have strengths (which are the things we are naturally good at) and weaknesses (which are the areas in which we are challenged to become stronger). This means that you should also start out expecting not to be perfect and knowing that you will make mistakes. Failure is a great way to learn because it teaches us what not to do.

You should expect that your success will require *hard work*. Learning a new skill is not easy, and it can be frustrating. Have you ever tried to learn to ride a bicycle? Do you remember falling again and again? Learning new things takes hard work.

You should also expect to *practice*. Let's use learning to play basketball as an example. You might know what you need to do to get the ball in the hoop, but you need to practice to improve at actually doing it. Even when you are great at it, you will occasionally miss a shot. We grow stronger by aiming for improvement, not perfection.

We learn to overcome challenges with hard work and practice. If this doesn't sound like fun, just remember how great it feels to ride that bicycle or land that free throw.

This book is especially for you, so let's see which skills are most important for you to work on. Then you can focus more on those skills to build your success. Take the quiz on the next few pages to get a better understanding of your strengths and weaknesses.

POWERS AND CHALLENGES

Let's start with some questions to determine in which situations you feel powerful and in which ones you might want some improvement. Answer the following questions by circling "Never," "Sometimes," "Often," or "Always."

1. Cleaning my room is hard. I usually need help to finish cleaning my room.

    Never   Sometimes   Often   Always

2. I need lots of reminders from my sidekicks to keep me on track with my homework.

    Never   Sometimes   Often   Always

3. My teacher tells me to pay attention.

    Never   Sometimes   Often   Always

4. It's hard for me to sit still in class.

    Never   Sometimes   Often   Always

5. When I feel grumpy or sad, I don't even know why I feel that way.

    Never   Sometimes   Often   Always

6. I don't notice when I am tired or hungry until someone tells me.

    Never   Sometimes   Often   Always

7. When I have a big project to do for school, I don't know how to get started and what to do each day.

    Never   Sometimes   Often   Always

8. Getting ready for school in the morning is a big challenge.

Never   Sometimes   Often   Always

9. When I am angry, I tend to yell, throw things, hit, or kick.

Never   Sometimes   Often   Always

10. I get in trouble when I don't mean to, like when I get too excited.

Never   Sometimes   Often   Always

11. I give up when something gets too frustrating or boring.

Never   Sometimes   Often   Always

12. I have a lot of half-finished projects, such as artworks or LEGO sets that never got completed.

Never   Sometimes   Often   Always

13. My room is pretty messy.

Never   Sometimes   Often   Always

14. I lose little things, like my socks or my pencils.

Never   Sometimes   Often   Always

15. I get in trouble at school for doing things impulsively, such as getting out of my chair or talking in class.

Never   Sometimes   Often   Always

16. I interrupt people when they are speaking even though I don't mean to.

Never   Sometimes   Often   Always

17. I need some help remembering what items to bring to school or to an activity.

Never   Sometimes   Often   Always

18. When I am going to an activity, I often run late or am the last one to get ready.

Never   Sometimes   Often   Always

19. I wait to do my chores or homework until the last minute.

Never   Sometimes   Often   Always

20. I might need to be told to do something a few times before I do it.

Never   Sometimes   Often   Always

Great job! Now let's talk about your strengths and challenges. If you answered mostly "always," you may be struggling with your executive functioning skills, but that's okay. This book can help. If you answered mostly "never," you may only need help with a few skills. Check out the Exercise Index on page 113 for the exercises that will help you improve the specific skills you find challenging.

BUILDING MY SKILLS

There are many awesome things that you can do to turn your executive functioning skill challenges into executive functioning skill superpowers. This book is going to give you tools and exercises to help you improve your skills, so you can feel more in control of whatever you have to do—whether it's taking charge of your homework, remembering your uniform for a soccer game, or playing with your friends.

This book has different chapters for situations at home, in school, and out in the world, but executive functioning skills work together across all the different areas of our daily lives. This means, for example, that you can use exercises or tips from the school chapter when you're at home or out in the world. In fact, you can use your creative, powerful mind to use any of these skills anywhere you find them helpful.

Every time you strengthen a new executive functioning skill, it is like gaining a new superpower. The exercises, tips, and tools offered in this book are like gadgets that activate these superpowers. It's time to show you how to find the right tools to make your superpowers work. Soon you will be able to identify and take better control of the troublesome or scattered parts of your life.

MY SUPERHERO TOOL VAULT

Before we show you any of those tools, however, let's create a vault for you to keep them in. Decorate the outside of your vault here. You can use colored pencils, crayons, stickers, glitter glue, or anything else you like to make this tool vault your own. Have fun and be creative. Leave the middle blank for now. You'll come back and draw gadgets as you learn new skills!

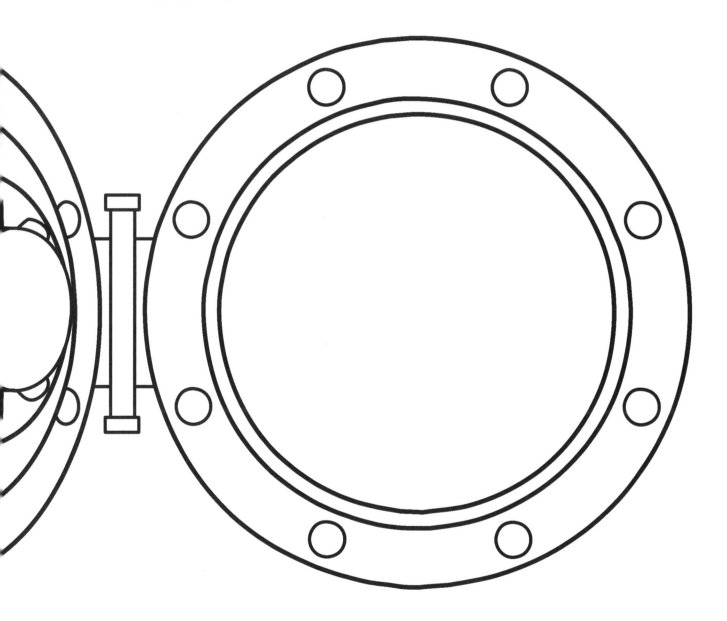

MY FIRST WORK SPACE

Whether it's a cave, a fortress, or an invisible airplane, all superheroes need a space of their own. Having your own neat and organized space will help you find your items. Work with a sidekick to create your own space. It could be as simple as a desk, a table, or even a box with a lid on it. Make sure everyone knows that this space is for you.

Think about what you want to put in your work space. Choose from the items below and add your own to design your work space. Look at this list each day to make sure you have all the things you need to use every day and that your work space is not getting cluttered with items you don't use very much.

What items do you want in your work space? Circle what you need from the items below and then add some of your own. Once you've made your plan, you're ready to set up your hideaway.

_____'s Work Space

Your name

Calculator	**Pencil sharpener**
Calendar	**Pencils**
Crayons	**Pens**
Glue sticks	**Ruler**
Paper	**Stapler**
Paper clips	**Sticky notes**

CREATE A VISION BOARD

What do you want to achieve with your superpowers? What does success look like to you? What does it feel like?

Cut out words and pictures from magazines or print out pictures from the Internet that describe your goals and how you will feel once you have achieved them. Maybe you can find a picture of a kid focusing on their homework or winning an award at school. Whatever you think of when you think about success belongs on this page. Paste the words and pictures in a collage below.

_____'s Vision Board
Your name

CHAPTER 3

Me at School

FOCUSING IN THE CLASSROOM

Elara is a third grader who is often told to focus in the classroom. "Focus!" says the line leader when Elara moves out of the line. "Focus!" says her teacher when Elara is working on her math sheets. "Focus!" says her music teacher when Elara is playing the recorder. Elara doesn't understand why so many people are telling her to focus. She focuses all the time. She focuses on the sounds of the birds outside, on the interesting objects around her, and on her thoughts about how to bake the largest cupcake ever. Why is everyone always telling Elara to focus? What is focus anyway?

Focus is how we take in and understand the things that are going on in our environment. There are a few different kinds of focus, and using them correctly can be a big help.

Selective focus is when we focus on one thing in our environment and block out everything else. Focusing on what your friend is saying while you are both on a noisy playground is an example of selective focus. You block out other noises so you can focus on your friend's voice.

Divided focus occurs when we are doing two things at the same time. Sometimes it is helpful, like when you talk with your friends and write down notes during a group project. Sometimes it does not work very well, like when are trying to remember the words to a song during a reading lesson.

Sustained focus is what we use when we are working on a single task for a long time. This kind of focus is also called attention span. Our attention span determines how long we can stay focused when working on a project.

HELP ELARA FIND HER FOCUS

Can you help Elara choose the right kind of focus to get her through her day? Draw an arrow from each task to the type of focus you think she will need.

Elara chats with her teacher while getting her notebook out of her backpack.

Selective Focus

Elara gets her art project and her art supplies from her cubby in the classroom.

Elara's teacher tells the class to work on their art project for the next 20 minutes.

Divided Focus

Elara's teacher reads them a story about a famous artist.

Elara chooses a book to read from the classroom's bookshelves.

Elara finishes a group project while chatting with her friends.

Sustained Focus

Elara listens to her teacher and ignores the kids playing outside near the classroom window.

WHOLE-BODY LISTENING

Anyone can listen with their ears, but a true superpower is being able to listen with your whole body. When you listen with your whole body, your power of focus is supercharged. Let's learn a song to help us do this.

To listen with our whole body, our head, shoulders, knees, and toes should be facing the speaker. Our eyes should be looking at their face. We listen with selective focus to their voice and to the words they are saying. In the classroom, you can use whole-body listening by sitting quietly at your desk, facing your teacher.

You can use the song "Head, Shoulders, Knees, and Toes" to help you remember how to listen with your whole body. We'll change the lyrics just a little bit.

Head, shoulders, knees, and toes, knees and toes

Head, shoulders, knees, and toes, knees and toes

Look and listen, that's how it goes

Head, shoulders, knees, and toes, knees and toes

PLANNING AND PRIORITIZING MY SCHOOL CALENDAR

Ryan is an amazing football player, top video game scorer, and all-around great friend. He wants to do well in school but is often surprised by quizzes that he didn't remember to prepare for. Does this ever happen to you? If it does, then you know how frustrating that can be.

Planning and prioritizing are skills that help us be proactive rather than reactive. When we are reactive, we react to things after they happen, just like a superhero who tries to catch a villain after he robbed a store. When we are proactive, we know what will happen and we make a plan. For instance, a superhero who is proactive knows that the villain is coming, makes a clever plan, and waits at the store to catch him in the act. As you can imagine, it is much easier and more efficient to be proactive.

CREATING MY SCHOOL CALENDAR, PART 1

An awesome homemade calendar can help you become proactive in your own life.

A calendar helps us plan and prioritize. It also helps us become proactive instead of reactive. With a calendar, we will be ready for anything. A school calendar should include school goals or events that do not occur every day, like tests, project due dates, or special events. You don't need to include things that are part of your daily routine, like catching the school bus.

You can use the next page to create and decorate a school calendar of your own. Place important events in the square that matches the day they will happen. You will need a new page for every month. You can buy a calendar, print one that is online, or even draw one. If you draw your own, make sure you include the year, the month, the date, and the days of the week.

MAY 2022

SUNDAY	MONDAY	TUESDAY	WEDNESDAY	THURSDAY	FRIDAY	SATURDAY
1	2	3	4	5	6	7
8	9	10	11 Math Test long division	12	13	14
15	16	17	18	19	20	21
22	23 School party Bring cupcakes	24	25	26	27 School ends early 12:00	28
29	30	31				

Month:			Year:			

CREATING MY SCHOOL CALENDAR, PART 2

You did an awesome job creating your calendar. You are now ready for advanced calendar training to build superpower skills in thoughtful planning and prioritizing.

Take a close look at each one of the events on your calendar. Do you need to do anything to plan for each of them? Perhaps you need to study for a test, read a book for a project, or bake cupcakes for a party.

A list of things we do to help us reach our goals is called an action plan, and we will learn more about action plans later in this chapter. Are there any actions that you should take in the days before your events to help you be successful? Note them on your calendar now.

Great job creating your action plans! Review your calendar every day for reminders of what to do today and for what is coming up tomorrow. When the month is over, make another calendar for the next month.

MAY 2022

SUNDAY	MONDAY	TUESDAY	WEDNESDAY	THURSDAY	FRIDAY	SATURDAY
1	2	3	4	5	6	7
8	9	10 Study for math test	11 Math Test long division	12	13	14
15	16	17	18	19	20	21
22 Bake cupcakes	23 School party Bring cupcakes	24	25	26	27 School ends early 12:00	28
29	30	31				

ORGANIZING MY SCHOOL LIFE

Mariko is a supersmart girl. She is a great reader and is able to do math better than anyone in her class. Her family can't understand why a smart girl like Mariko is always losing and forgetting things.

Mariko is struggling with organization. Organization is the skill that helps you arrange your things in an orderly fashion so that you can keep track of them. Mariko is so busy thinking about supersmart things that she doesn't always pay attention to what she is doing or where she is placing her important items. When this happens, she gets a visit from the Scatterer. The Scatterer hides things and makes a mess. Let's look at an example.

On Tuesday, Mariko's teacher told the students to turn in their homework and take out their math notebooks. Mariko looked for her homework, but she'd forgotten to put it in her backpack. Mariko was worried about her missing homework. She took her notebook out for the lesson, but she was so busy worrying that she didn't notice that she'd accidentally grabbed her reading notebook instead of her math notebook. As her teacher started the lesson, Mariko realized her mistake. She tried to quietly grab the right notebook and find her pencil, which was buried somewhere in her backpack. Mariko's teacher looked at her and wondered why Mariko was taking so long to get started.

Can you imagine how Mariko was feeling? Have you ever struggled with organization? If you have, it's okay. Let's look at some tools you can use to build the superpower of organization.

SECRET CODES

Color coding is a super tool to help you get organized in school. Decide on a color for each of your subjects and ask your sidekick to help you get notebooks and folders to match each one. You might choose to have a green notebook and folder for math and red ones for reading. You can use a marker or highlighter to color around the edges of the notebook pages so the whole notebook is that color. That will make it much easier to find it in your desk, cubby, or book bag. Make sure you label each item with your name and the proper subject.

You can design your color code here using the notebooks shown.

LABELS

Being organized means keeping things in the same place all the time. Labels remind us of where everything goes so we can practice this skill. It's really fun to make labels, and you can use them in your backpack, your desk, your cubby, your work space . . . practically anywhere! You can use a marker or stickers to make your labels. Just make sure that if you are labeling school property you have permission to do so.

Take a look at some of these areas that you might use at school. Write down what you think should go in each section. Use the words from the list below to start, then add your own if there's anything else you bring to school every day.

Coat	Homework	Ruler
Crayons	Lunch	Water
Folders	Notebooks	
Glue	Pencil box	

Desk	Cubby	Lunch Box	Backpack

Now that you have made a plan, ask your sidekick to help you try it in real life. Try labeling each pocket of your backpack so that you know where everything is supposed to go. What else can you label?

WORKING INDEPENDENTLY IN SCHOOL

Have you noticed that being successful in school means more than just being good at math or science? Kids in school have a lot of things to do. You need to listen, cooperate, and take turns. You need to know when it's okay to raise your hand and speak and when it's better to be silent. You need to follow the teacher's instructions and keep your hands and feet quiet. This is all part of working independently. Working independently means knowing what to do and what not to do without being told.

Sebastian is a student helper in the third grade. He and his friends spend one hour a week in the kindergarten class, helping the younger kids learn how to get along with one another and power up their school performance. They use songs and worksheets to teach the kindergartners what to do and what to avoid in different situations. For instance, they teach them that when walking in the hallway, they should stay in line, listen to their teacher, and avoid bumping into one another.

Sebastian and his friends think about how they could work independently to power up their own performance. For example, they think that if they want to learn how to do long division, they need to listen to the teacher, pay attention to the examples, and avoid talking with others. If they want to take a test successfully, they need to be calm and focused, read the questions carefully, and avoid rushing. Do you know what to do and what not to do to power up your success in school?

MY SCHOOL PLAN FOR TODAY

For each of the situations on the next page, choose two items from the "What to do" list and one item from the "What to avoid" list below. There are no right answers, and you may use items more than once—just choose the ones that you think are most important for you.

What to do:

Ask for help

Be kind

Drink water

Listen

Raise hand

Read carefully

Share

Sit quietly

Take a breath

Take my time

Take turns

Walk quietly

Watch the teacher

What to avoid:

Daydream

Get out of my seat

Get too close

Hit or kick

Hog the ball

Interrupt

Look out the window

Poke or pinch

Put my head down

Rush

Talk

Tease others

Yell

Working on a math sheet

What to do:

....

....

What to avoid:

....

Quiet reading time

What to do:

....

....

What to avoid:

....

Entering the classroom

What to do:

....

....

What to avoid:

....

Lunchtime

What to do:

....

....

What to avoid:

....

Gym class

What to do:

....

....

What to avoid:

....

Taking a test

What to do:

....

....

What to avoid:

....

TOLERATING BOREDOM

Feeling bored can make it hard to keep listening or working. What does boredom feel like to you? Does it make you feel antsy or like you are in slow motion? Draw your boredom here:

Try this trick at school. Put this chart on your desk. For each subject during the day, write an X in the box on the same row of the subject every time you feel bored. Then take a deep breath and try to keep working. Imagine how you'll feel when you've successfully finished with the lesson. See how many Xs each subject earns. Be proud of yourself for continuing to work, especially in subjects with lots of Xs.

	SUN	MON	TUE	WED	THU	FRI	SAT
Math							
English Language Arts							
Science							
Social Studies							

Do you like this chart? Make copies of it and try it every day for a week.

BEING GOAL-ORIENTED

Being goal-oriented means choosing a goal and sticking with it. Of course, not everyone has the same goals. For instance, your friend might want to make the softball team, your brother might want to get good grades, and you might want to win the school's art contest.

Being goal-oriented is challenging, because it means sticking with your goal even when you become frustrated or discouraged. Juliane was a second grader who wanted to read a chapter book by herself. Sometimes she needed to read sentences or paragraphs twice to understand what she was reading, and it took her a long time to get through each chapter. Juliane set a goal to read the book for 15 minutes every day. Some days she did not feel like reading, but she read anyway. Some days she felt frustrated or bored with the book, but she read anyway. Juliane read every day until she finally finished the book. Finishing the book made Juliane feel happy and proud.

MY ACTION PLAN

An action plan is a handy tool that you can use to set goals and achieve them. With an action plan, it's better to focus on one goal at a time. Once you complete a goal, you can start working on another one. Jung was struggling with his math skills and wanted to improve them. He asked his teacher for help. His teacher suggested that Jung make a detailed action plan. So, Jung set a specific goal for himself to get a B on the next math test. Then, he thought about what actions he could take to achieve that goal. He decided to do a math worksheet every day. That is more specific than if he just decided he would practice more math. Lastly, Jung measured his progress. He put an X on the calendar for each day he completed a worksheet. When he took his next math test, he got a B+ and felt enormously proud of himself.

Now, you can develop your own action plan. Once you write out your action plan, make sure you check it every day so you can mark your progress.

For this plan, let's focus on a school goal. What is something you would like to achieve at school? Be specific.

Develop your action plan here:

GOAL

....

ACTION PLAN

....

REWARD

....

ADDING MY NEW TOOLS TO THE VAULT

You have done an amazing job so far learning about the tools and tricks you can use to power up your executive functioning skills. Which tools and tricks do you like the most? Go back to your superhero tool vault (page 26) and draw your favorite tools in the vault.

Try to imagine these tools as "gadgets" and give each of them a cool new name. For instance, you can rename color coding (page 40) as superhero spray paint. Give them each a name that you love and will be easy for you to remember.

CHAPTER 4

Me at Home

MANAGING MY TIME

Amelia sat at her desk to do her homework. What was her homework? Hmm . . . she remembered there was a math sheet. She thought there was something else, too. She thought about it for a while. "Amelia, do your homework," said her mom. Amelia couldn't find a pencil. She got up to get one. While she was looking for a pencil, she saw her sister playing with a new game. "Can I play, too?" asked Amelia. "Amelia, do your homework," said her mom. Amelia got a pencil and passed the kitchen on the way back. She realized she was thirsty and grabbed a drink of water. She sat down at the table to drink the water and thought about maybe going to the beach the next day. "Amelia!" said her mom. "What are you doing? I told you to do your homework!"

Amelia is having difficulty managing her time. If her day keeps going the same way, she might find herself still needing to do homework at bedtime. Managing time is a skill that allows us to use our time effectively and get things done.

There are several things that can steal away our time. Time stealers include things like hunger, thirst, confusion, distraction, and disorganization. When we learn to manage these obstacles, we can work more efficiently and accomplish a lot. For instance, imagine if Amelia had gotten herself a snack before she sat down to do her homework, taken out her planner so she knew exactly what homework was required, and then found her pencil right away. Do you think she would have finished her homework more quickly?

THE TIME BANDITS

Sometimes when you are trying to do something important like homework, the Time Bandits strike. They will try to steal away your time. Look at the list of Time Bandits below and check off any that are causing you problems. Then, write down a way to stop each Time Bandit.

Hint: a successful solution tells you what to do, instead of what *not* to do. For instance, it is better to say, "I will go to a quieter space" rather than, "I will not socialize." See if you can find solutions to stop each of your Time Bandits. When you are done, ask your sidekick what they think about your brilliant plan.

	The Time Bandits	How I Can Stop This Time Bandit
Distracted Body	○ I'm hungry	
	○ I'm thirsty	
	○ I'm tired	
	○ I'm fidgety	

	The Time Bandits	How I Can Stop This Time Bandit
Distracted Mind	○ **I'm distracted by noise in my environment**	
	○ **I'm socializing**	
	○ **I'm daydreaming**	
	○ **I'm trying to rush**	
	○ **I'm texting, looking at my phone, or playing with my computer or tablet**	
Disorganization	○ **I don't know what I'm supposed to do (I don't know my goal)**	
	○ **I don't know how to start**	
	○ **I don't know how to do the task**	
	○ **My papers or binders are messy**	
	○ **I can't find the paper or the materials I need**	

TIME-GUESSING GAME

Do you have an idea how long it takes you to do things? For instance, how quickly can you get dressed? Or make a sandwich? Or clean your room? Learning how long things take helps us power up our time-management skills.

Start by choosing any task at all. Guess how long you think it will take you to do it. Then set the timer and see if you can get it done (correctly) before the timer goes off. If you didn't complete the task within the time you guessed, that's okay. Just consider how much more time you think you will need, set the timer, and try again.

Now, give it a try with the tasks below.

Water the plants

_____ minutes

Build a two-foot-tall tower with LEGO bricks

_____ minutes

Draw a picture of your family

_____ minutes

Complete a math sheet

_____ minutes

Read a book chapter

_____ minutes

Vacuum the living room

_____ minutes

Great job! What other things can you time?

AVOIDING DISTRACTIONS

Koda loves theater and is thrilled when he gets the lead role in the school play. He takes his script home and starts memorizing his lines, but he is soon set upon by the League of Distractors. "Drip drop!" goes the sink faucet distractor. "Vroom!" is the sound made by the garbage truck distractor as it passes by outside. The television distractor in the next room starts murmuring about the weekend weather. A distractor in Koda's stomach is grumbling, and a thought distractor keeps wondering if he is going to choose the yellow or green highlighter. How will Koda ever get his lines memorized?

Distractors live in lots of places in our homes and can make it very hard to get things done. When we are in charge of our focus, we get to choose what we want to do and successfully complete the task. A distractor is anything that takes away our focus and makes it difficult to succeed. Distractors might include distracting sights, such as a messy tabletop or your dog being especially cute. They may include sounds, such as the television, kids playing outside, or someone talking in the next room. We can also be distracted by our own thoughts or feelings, such as hunger, thirst, or the decision about what to do next. Some people don't notice distractors very much, but other people find them extremely annoying.

If you find it hard to focus when distractors are around, you may notice that you have a harder time with tasks that require focus and concentration. Use the following exercises to help you build up the superpower of staying focused.

A VISIT TO THE LABORATORY

Let's take a visit to a laboratory, where you will find lots of gadgets that can power up your ability to focus and concentrate. Like a scientist working in a lab, you may need to test these gadgets out to see if they'll work for you. These may be objects you already have in your home or items you may consider getting or creating for yourself. Circle the items you think would be helpful to you. Once you are done, you can color and decorate the laboratory.

Action plan   **Neat work area**

Chewing gum   **Phone/tablet turned off**

Comfortable clothes   **Soft music**

Earplugs   **Timer**

Fan   **Water**

Fidget toy   **Weighted blanket**

Healthy snacks   **White noise machine**

THE INVISIBLE SHIELD

When you need to concentrate on a task, you can use an invisible shield to create a bubble of protection around you to help keep you focused. Create your invisible shield each time you are about to begin a task that requires focus and concentration. Create your shield by connecting the dots below, then color it in and decorate it.

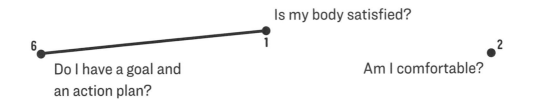

Is my body satisfied?

6   1   2

Do I have a goal and an action plan?   Am I comfortable?

5   Do I have all the things I need?   Is the room quiet? 3

4

Is the room visually calm and clear?

TAKING CHARGE OF HOUSEHOLD TASKS

Alani and her sister, Kaia, both have chores to do each week at home. It's Alani's chore to set the table, and Kaia helps her dad dry the dishes. Alani takes out the garbage, and Kaia feeds the dog. Alani and Kaia both keep their rooms clean and make their beds each morning.

Like lots of kids, Alani has a hard time starting and completing tasks. In fact, she often gets in trouble for not listening. Alani is not sure why she sometimes needs to be told two or three times to do something. Has this ever happened to you?

What makes starting tasks so difficult? Starting tasks often means we have to switch from doing one thing to another. It may even mean switching from doing something we like, such as playing outside, to something we don't like, such as setting the table. This is not always easy to do. Completing tasks can also be challenging, because it requires keeping our focus on what we are doing and having persistence. Luckily, there are some ways to power up these skills.

Our next two exercises will help us power up the skills of starting and completing tasks.

ROCKET SHIP COUNTDOWN

Getting started on a task can be hard. Sometimes, it's easy to get overwhelmed by everything you need to do. Look at the tasks below and think about the very first thing you'd need to do to get started on each task. For example, if you're doing homework, the first step might be finding a pencil or getting your worksheet out of your backpack. Write down your very first step next to each task. Then, add some more of your tasks and their first steps.

Set the table for dinner: ....

Clean your room: ....

Get ready for bed: ....

Start your homework: ....

Take out the garbage: ....

Load the dishwasher: ....

Get ready for school: ....

.... : ....

.... : ....

.... : ....

Here's an idea: Whenever you need to start a new task, picture being an astronaut on a rocket ship. Think about how astronauts know that the countdown means their rocket ship is about to launch. It gives them time to take a deep breath and get ready. Why don't you try counting down from 10 the next time you have to start a new task? Think about your first step, take a deep breath, and get started.

10, 9, 8, 7, 6, 5, 4, 3, 2, 1, Liftoff!

FAMILY CONTROL CENTER

You can help your whole family complete tasks. Use the sample chart as an example and fill in the blank chart to create a family control center of your own. At the top of the column, write the person's name. On the next row, write a reward that they would like to achieve. An example of a reward might be watching a movie, playing a game, or eating an ice cream cone. On the bottom square, write down the task they need to complete each day. You can add more columns for more people, if needed. Every time each person completes their task, they get a check mark. When they get 10 check marks, they get their reward. Now they can choose another reward and start again.

It's okay if someone misses a check mark one day. Not everyone will move at the same pace. If you don't get your check mark, you can just try again tomorrow.

Name: Dad	Name: Me	Name: Sister
Reward: Breakfast in bed	Reward: Movie night	Reward: Swim in the lake
	✓	
	✓	✓
✓	✓	✓
✓	✓	✓
Task: Clean the kitchen	Task: Take out the garbage	Task: Feed the dog

Name:	Name:	Name:	Name:	Name:
Reward:	Reward:	Reward:	Reward:	Reward:
Task:	Task:	Task:	Task:	Task:

SELF-REGULATING HOMEWORK AND TEST PREPARATION

Superhero, you are doing a great job! We are ready to promote you to the more complex skills of studying and tackling your homework from start to finish. Now, you might be a superhero, but you are also a kid, so let's make sure we get some help from your sidekicks.

Have you ever seen a superhero in battle? Does a superhero use only one move over and over or a combination of moves? Superheroes may use a combination of flying, punching, lifting heavy objects, and outsmarting their foe to win a battle. Similarly, a basketball player needs to know how to combine running, jumping, dribbling, and throwing to play ball.

Can you think of something you are good at? What combination of skills makes you successful?

Executive functioning skills work the same way as many other skills. When we combine them, we make them more powerful. For instance, doing homework requires a combination of skills, such as thoughtful planning, time management, organization, and focus. It's helpful to make tasks a little more fun and interesting by playing games like the Time-Guessing Game (Exercise 22). The next two exercises will teach you a fun game to help you study and show you how to combine some of your powerful techniques for homework success.

MEMORY GAME

This is a game that you can use when studying. You will need eight note cards or two sheets of paper cut into four equal pieces each.

On one side of the card, write a word or concept. On the other side, write what you need to know about it. For instance, a vocabulary word can go on the front side, and its definition can go on the back.

Place your eight finished cards in a pile with the word or concept side up. Look at each card one by one and see if you can get the right answer. If you guess correctly, place it in a Correct pile. If you guess incorrectly, place it in a Try Again pile. When you are finished, take the cards in the Try Again pile and try again. Keep doing this until all your cards land in the Correct pile.

Then ask your sidekick to test you and see if you can get them all correct again.

THE HOMEWORK LADDER OF SUCCESS

Now, let's put our skills together and climb the ladder of success. Then, color in the picture on the next page.

1.   Initiation. Get ready for liftoff (Exercise 25).

2.   Create your invisible shield (Exercise 24).

3.   Organize your work space (Exercise 16).

4.   Check your calendar. Add anything new to it now (Exercises 13 and 14).

5.   Create your action plan (Exercise 19).

6.   Guess how long each assignment will take and set the timer (Exercise 22). Be sure to take a breath, stretch, and drink some water between homework assignments.

7.   Put all your homework in your backpack and use your clue card to make sure you have everything you need for tomorrow (Exercise 3).

8.   Enjoy the feeling of success.

MANAGING MY EMOTIONS WITH MY FAMILY

The day that Stef got mad at her brother George was just after her ninth birthday. Stef was trying to play her new video game, and George wanted to play, too. When Stef told George he couldn't play, he started distracting her on purpose and ruining the game. Stef got frustrated and yelled at him. When that didn't work, she bumped her elbow into him, just a little. George screamed and then ran to tell their grandma. When their grandma told Stef she couldn't play her game anymore, Stef was sad and angry. Her heart was pounding, her muscles were tense, and she felt like she might cry. Instead, she yelled at her grandma and stomped upstairs. "It isn't fair!" she shouted. Then she ran into her brother's room and threw one of his toys into the garbage.

Can you imagine how Stef was feeling? What do you think about the choices she made? Would you have made any different ones?

We all have different ways that we respond to our emotions. Some are helpful, like naming the emotions, crying, and talking about them. Some are not so helpful, like yelling, hitting, or running away. The not-so-helpful responses often happen when our emotions get big and we feel out of control. One way we can manage our way through them is by simply taking a break. During the break we can draw, practice breathing, exercise, or simply relax. These techniques help calm our emotions so that we can think more clearly and make smarter choices.

TAKE A BREAK CARDS

Let's make some heart-shaped Take a Break cards that you can use at home. Keep the cards somewhere in your home where you can easily get to them when you need them. When you notice your emotions getting big, hand one of the cards to a grown-up to let them know you need to take a break. Go to your room or a quiet place away from everyone else and set the timer for 10 minutes. Your sidekicks can also help you know when you need a break. If they see your emotions getting big, they can hand you a card. Then, you can take a break to feel better and get control over your emotions again.

Take a piece of plain paper or construction paper and draw a heart on it.

Cut out the heart and write the words *Take a Break* on it. Then decorate it however you like. Make several of them to store away for when you might need them.

ADDING MORE TOOLS TO MY VAULT

Let's revisit your superhero tool vault (page 26). Are there any new exercises, tips, or tools that have helped you? If so, draw your new tools in your vault. Don't forget to label them with your own creative gadget names.

CHAPTER 5

Me in the World

BEING FLEXIBLE

Mental flexibility is our ability to adapt our behaviors in response to changes in the environment. Imagine that you go outside one morning, and it is quite cold out. You might decide to put on a coat. As you start walking, the clouds move away from the sun and it becomes much warmer. What do you think you might do? Would you take off your coat? This is an example of mental flexibility. You changed what you did in response to changes in your environment.

Mental flexibility is handy for all sorts of things. It allows us to choose a new snack if we run out of our favorite. It helps us change our plans: For instance, if we were planning to go to the museum but find out it is closed, we can go to the zoo instead. It also helps us switch tasks, like when we move from reading to math, to lunch, and to gym. Mental flexibility reduces frustration, because instead of being "locked" into an idea or a behavior, we can easily move from one thing to the next.

People who have strong mental flexibility can "go with the flow." If plans change, they just adapt and adjust to the new plan. If you are easily able to change plans or switch tasks, it means your mental flexibility skills are strong. If you struggle with this, don't worry. Mental flexibility is a skill you can practice and power up.

WHAT WOULD I DO?

Did you know there is more than one right way of thinking about things? Imagine that your dad wants you to do your homework because he feels that good grades are important. Maybe you don't want to do your homework because you think homework is boring. Flexible thinking lets us see the situation from both perspectives and understand that they are both correct. When we use mental flexibility, it helps us control our emotions and think before we act.

Look at the situations below. Each one requires some flexible thinking. For each situation, write or draw at least two different ways you could react.

You miss a goal in your soccer game.

<table>
<tr><td></td><td></td></tr>
</table>

Your class is supposed to go on a field trip to a farm, but it's raining out, so the trip is canceled.

You're on a long car trip with your family and feel very bored.

CHANGE THE ENDING

Plans change all the time. When we make a plan, we expect a certain ending to our story. For instance, if we plan to bake a cake after school, we look forward to starting by mixing the batter and ending by eating the finished cake with our family. Flexible thinking allows us to imagine a new story or possibility if the plan changes.

Think of a movie you've seen many times. First, write about how the movie ends on the lines below.

....

....

....

....

....

....

....

....

....

....

....

....

Now, imagine that the director of the movie told you that they no longer want to use that ending. They need your creative mind to help them come up with a new ending. Can you use your mental flexibility skills to imagine a different ending to the story?

....

....

....

....

....

....

....

....

....

....

....

....

....

....

CONTROLLING MY IMPULSES

Kirima is excited because her mom is taking her to Shelly's Candy Store for the very first time. Shelly's is famous for having almost every kind of candy you can imagine. The store is packed with giant lollipops, chocolate bars, little caramels, taffies, and gummies. There is chewing gum, sour balls, powder sticks, and candy that pops on your tongue.

Kirima's eyes go wide the second she steps inside Shelly's. She wants to grab every piece of candy she can and try them all. Instead, she remembers that her mom said she could only have three pieces of candy. It takes Kirima a while to decide which three she wants, but eventually she chooses just three. Her mom pays for the treats, and Kirima holds the bag calmly without even trying to sneak a quick bite of candy. As Kirima and her mom leave the shop, Shelly praises Kirima for being so well behaved.

Have you ever noticed that the world is a tempting place? There are so many things to touch, see, say, and do. Have you ever wanted to roll around on a fuzzy carpet? Or interrupt someone who is talking to tell them a great story? Or even poke your friend? What do you think would happen if you followed every impulse you had?

Response inhibition is a skill that allows us to be aware of what we are thinking and then stop an impulse if it is not appropriate. For instance, response inhibition stops us from talking out loud in class and reminds us to raise our hand first. You can imagine it as a big red stop sign inside your brain. It allows us to remember to do important things like put on a helmet before riding a bike, wait for our turn, or be patient with a younger sibling.

GAMES TO LEARN BY

Do you want to practice response inhibition? Here are some games you can play to make your response inhibition powers stronger.

SIMON SAYS

Choose a leader who will act as "Simon." The leader tells and shows the other players what to do. The trick is to do whatever the leader says only if they say, "Simon says" first. So, if the leader says, "Simon says clap your hands," you should clap your hands. If the leader says, "Tap your feet," you should not tap your feet because Simon didn't say to do it.

FREEZE TAG

One person is "it." The person who is "it" tries to tag everyone else. If you get tagged, you are frozen. You must stay perfectly still until another player taps you and unfreezes you.

READING TOGETHER

Take turns reading a story with another person. You read a paragraph while they listen, and then they read a paragraph while you listen.

STOP

Have you ever been so busy feeling your feelings or thinking your thoughts that you forget to observe what is happening around you? Sometimes we may be playing outside, and we are having so much fun that we forget to lower our voices or calm our bodies when we come inside. Sometimes we are so busy saying something that we don't hear the teacher's instructions. This can happen anytime. We can use the STOP exercise throughout our day to help us observe what is happening and make appropriate choices.

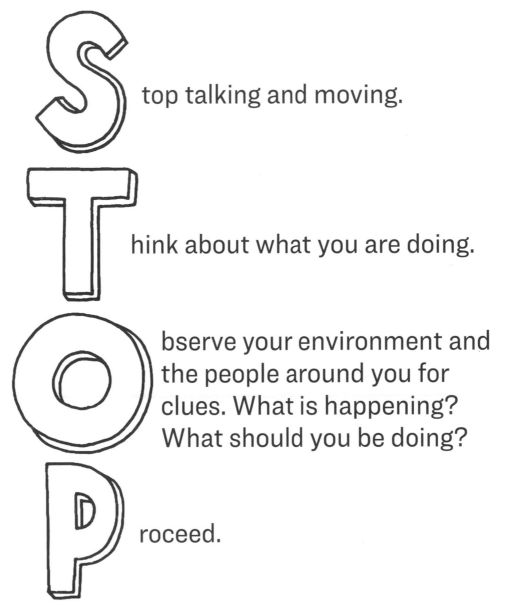

S top talking and moving.

T hink about what you are doing.

O bserve your environment and the people around you for clues. What is happening? What should you be doing?

P roceed.

CONTROLLING MY EMOTIONS WITH MY FRIENDS

Max was having a bad day. Max's best friend was absent from school, and he sat by himself on the bus feeling disappointed. Then Max's teacher gave them a surprise quiz, and Max felt sorry that he had not studied the material the night before. He worried about getting a bad grade. His classmate Ilene kept tap-tap-tapping her pencil, and Max felt himself becoming annoyed. "Stop it!" he told her in a grumpy voice. Max played tag with his friends at recess. When it was his turn to chase everyone, he became tired and frustrated. "I quit!" he yelled at his friends, and then stomped off to sit by himself.

Max was struggling to control his emotions. When his emotions got too big, he ended up being grumpy and yelling at his friends. Sometimes when our emotions get big, we might do other things, too, like cry, run away, say mean things, or even throw things, hit, or kick. When we lose control of our emotions, we often say and do things that we don't really mean. Do you think Max could have done anything differently? Have you ever lost control of your emotions with your friends? What was that like for you?

If you struggle with controlling your emotions, you are not alone. The good news is that we can *feel* our emotions, but we don't have to *act* on them. Instead, we can learn to observe them, think about them, and talk about them. It isn't easy, but with time and practice, you can build this superpower.

NAME THE EMOTION

Understanding and sharing emotions is a powerful tool for getting along with others. When we have a strong emotion, we can tell a helper or a friend how we feel. Naming our emotions and telling other people how we feel can keep us calm and in control. Do you know the meaning of emotions? Can you draw faces to match the emotions below?

Afraid

Jealous

Angry

Sad

Annoyed

Sorry

Disappointed

Surprised

Excited

Worried

Happy

THINK BEFORE SPEAKING

When we act on our emotions, we can sometimes say things we don't mean. Have you ever said anything that accidentally made someone feel sad, angry, or annoyed? Have your friends ever told you that you talk about your favorite subject too much when you are excited? How do we figure out if something is okay to say? We can use each of the letters in the word *think* to help us decide if it is a good idea to say what we are thinking.

Should I say it?

Is it . . .

T—true?

H—helpful?

I—important?

N—new?

K—kind?

Let's practice. Think about something you might say to your best friend. Write it down here:

....

Now, let's apply your new THINK tool:

Is it true?   **Yes   No**

Is it helpful?   **Yes   No**

Is it important?   **Yes   No**

Is it new?   **Yes   No**

Is it kind?   **Yes   No**

If you answered yes to all five questions, then it's a good idea to say what you're thinking. You can use this exercise anytime you're not sure if what you're thinking is okay to say out loud.

STARTING AND FINISHING ACTIVITIES

When it comes to spring cleaning in the garden, everyone in Omar's family has a job. His sister Yasmin digs holes for the new flowers, and his sister Noor plants the seeds. Omar's brother, Asad, pulls the weeds. As the youngest, it's Omar's job to pick up all the sticks before his father mows the lawn. Omar steps out of his house and takes a deep breath of the spring air. He looks over the lawn. A lot of big sticks and little twigs fell to the ground over the winter, and they are scattered everywhere. Omar pulls on his garden gloves and looks up at the sky. "Come on, Omar, let's get going," says Asad. Omar looks around the yard. Where to start? He picks up a few sticks, but it doesn't seem to make much of a difference. "How long will this take?" he wonders.

Omar struggles with starting and finishing activities. His family has noticed that he often has a hard time with chores, and they sometimes wonder if he is just trying to get out of work. In truth, Omar often doesn't know where to start and how to proceed, which makes it hard for him to keep going. Do you ever have a hard time knowing what to do during group activities? If so, it's okay. Use the exercises that come next to give you a hand.

A FEW OF MY FAVORITE THINGS

Getting started includes knowing what items you need to get ready. Let's imagine that you have something to do. What items would you need to get ready? Let's make a chart of three of your favorite activities and a list of the items you will need for each one.

Favorite activity 1:	Favorite activity 2:	Favorite activity 3:
What is it?	**What is it?**	**What is it?**
What do I need?	**What do I need?**	**What do I need?**

COUNTDOWN TO SUCCESS

Imagine that you had a playdate at a friend's house, and now it's time to help put away the toys. Counting items can be a fun way to measure your progress.

Simply count how many items there are and write that number down. If you like, you can each agree to clean up half the toys and both count as you go.

You can vary this game by counting something else, like colors. Count how many red things there are to clean up, then write the number down. Clean them up together, and count as you go until you have cleaned up every red thing. After that, count and put away the blue things, then the yellow things, and so on.

Another idea is to count categories. Count how many dolls need to be put away, how many balls need to be put away, or how many crayons need to be put away.

What else can you count?

PLANNING AND PRIORITIZING MY LIFE CALENDAR

Jada is so excited for summer. She is planning to see the fireworks for the Fourth of July and then start summer camp the very next morning. She will also be taking swim lessons, her cousins are planning a visit, and July 7 is her birthday party. And she has a weekly math tutoring session, which she isn't that excited about, but at least her tutor is super nice.

Going places, having special events, and keeping a busy schedule takes thoughtful planning. When planning, it can be helpful to use the 3 Ws: what, when, and where. What is Jada going to be doing? (go to summer camp) When is she going? (July 5 at 8 a.m.) Where will it be? (in the park)

The "what" tells Jada about the event, so that she can prepare properly. Jada knows that she wants to bring her baseball mitt and her camp T-shirt, so she should pack those things. The "when" tells Jada the day and time. Jada is leaving at 8:00 in the morning, which means she will not have time for a playdate that day. The "where" tells Jada the location. The camp is in the park, so Jada should also pack some bug spray.

Do you remember the school calendar you created in Exercises 13 and 14? Your world is much bigger and more exciting than just school. Let's create another calendar for whatever is happening in the rest of your world. Being prepared will help you be ready for anything.

MY BIG LIFE CALENDAR

Use this page (or you can purchase a calendar or even print one from the Internet) to mark down your special events, using the three Ws to help you along the way. Then add in anything else you need to be prepared, like Jada did.

Jada's Calendar

Month: July   **Year: 2021**

SUNDAY	MONDAY	TUESDAY	WEDNESDAY	THURSDAY	FRIDAY	SATURDAY
				1	2	3
4 Fireworks 7:00 Julianne Lane Park — Pack swimsuit and lunch for camp, set alarm	5 First Day of Camp 8:00 am bus	6 Math tutor 4:00 — Choose party clothes and get the backyard ready	7 My birthday party! 2:00 Backyard	8	9	10
11 4:00 Cousin visit	12	13 Math tutor 4:00	14	15	16	17
18	19	20 Math tutor 4:00	21	22	23	24 Cousin visit sleepover day 2
25	26	27 Math tutor 4:00	28	29	30	31

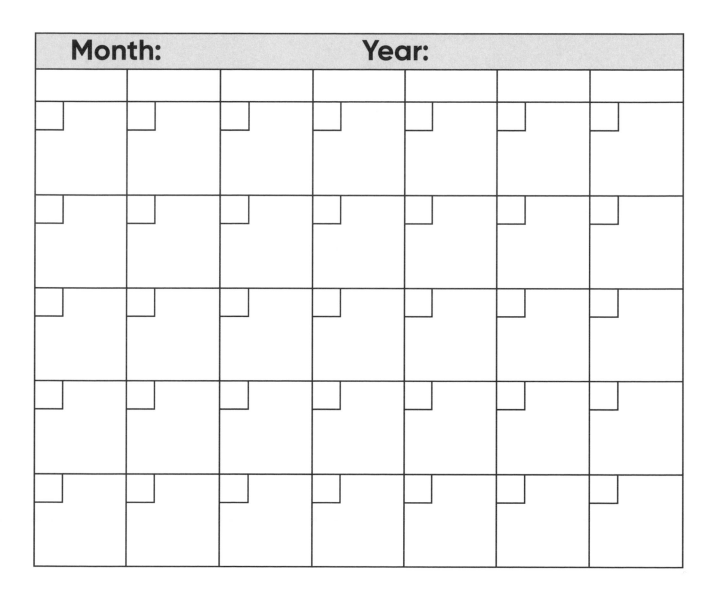

Month:			Year:			

COMPLETING MY TOOL VAULT

It's time to finish up your superhero tool vault. Choose the exercises, tips, and tools that have helped you the most from this section and draw them into your vault on page 26. Remember to label them and give them awesome superhero gadget names.

CHAPTER 6

Just for Parents

POSITIVE PARENTING AND EXECUTIVE FUNCTIONING SKILLS

Executive functioning skills are often a mystery to parents *and* children. It can be hard to fathom why a child might appear lazy or unmotivated, appear overly emotional, or struggle with tasks that don't stump other kids of the same age.

Let's begin with an understanding that neither the parents nor the child are to blame. Baseline executive functioning skills come from the neurological development of the frontal lobes of the brain. Stronger or weaker executive functioning skills are inherited, much like artistic or athletic talent. Plus, executive functioning skills continue to develop into adulthood. At ages 6 to 9 years, kids should not be expected to have completely mastered all these skills.

The good news is that executive functioning skills can improve, and there are some parenting techniques that can help you help your child. Positive parenting theory is very useful when it comes to managing difficult behaviors and encouraging new learning. It is based on the idea that there are no bad children, just good behaviors and bad behaviors. It centers on an approach that is honest, optimistic, and based on empathy and respect.

Positive parenting starts with the assumption that children have the desire to do the right thing. This makes a lot of intuitive sense, as we know that most children want to be praised and don't want to be labeled as disorganized, forgetful, emotional, or lazy.

What follows then is for parents to try to discover why the child is misbehaving. Some important questions to ask yourself are: "Is my child feeling listened to?" "Are my expectations reasonable?" and "Do they understand the reasoning behind my expectations?" Children who feel unheard, discouraged, or confused are more likely to misbehave. These conversations are important, but also remember that children may not always be able to explain their actions, and you may have to infer their reasons via your observations.

What can you do as parents to encourage your children and help improve their behaviors as you work on the exercises in this book? First, allow your children to experience a range of emotions, including difficult ones like boredom, anxiety, and fear. Validate that their feelings are important, even if you might not understand or agree with them. As parents, we don't need to rescue children from their emotions. Instead, we should teach them that feelings are temporary and that feelings don't need to control actions. They can survive all sorts of feelings and still be okay, and you can help.

Give your children lots of praise and acknowledge their efforts and their progress. Try to praise them at least three times more often than you correct them. Spend quality time with your kids and make an effort to understand and enjoy their interests.

Parenting is most effective when parents model the behaviors they want from their children. It is unreasonable to expect a behavior from a child that we are unable to do ourselves. Model kindness and respect, and do your best to refrain from yelling or name-calling. Be aware that being kind is not the same as being permissive. Engage in gentle but firm discipline, such as time-outs and removal of privileges, and plan to ignore negative behaviors. Children pay attention to our actions more than our words. Consistency and follow-through on limits are essential.

Manage your own expectations, too. Educate yourself about what misbehaviors are expected in children of different ages and treat every mistake and misbehavior as a learning occasion. Be aware that helping children takes time, patience, and lots of repetition. Children with executive functioning difficulties may need daily help with complex skills such as homework, cleaning, and time management until middle school or beyond.

Above all, engage in self-care. Parenting is a marathon, not a sprint. Take breaks and get help and support, including professional support, as needed. Acknowledge your own mistakes as an opportunity to learn and grow. And always be kind to yourself. This section will provide additional ideas to guide you through your parenting journey.

ASSESSING YOUR CHILD'S SKILLS

Here are a few questions you can ask yourself to determine if a particular skill is something your child would benefit from improving.

COMPLETING TASKS

Are your child's half-finished projects lying all over your house? How many times have LEGO sets or puzzles been out for a week or more because your child is still "finishing" them? Does your child struggle with picking up where they left off after taking a break?

CHOOSING GOALS AND STICKING TO THEM

When your child is working toward a goal, such as learning to ride a bicycle, do they keep trying? Or do they give up as soon as they become frustrated or bored? Do you feel that they can see the achievement ahead of them and are able to work their way toward it?

STAYING FOCUSED

Is your child a daydreamer? Does their teacher report that they are having difficulty paying attention in school? Do you notice at home that they often flit from one task to another? Or get easily distracted in conversation and have a hard time finishing an idea? Do you find yourself giving your child multiple prompts to stay on tasks such as homework?

CONTROLLING EMOTIONS

Is your child a big presence in your household? Do you find that other members of the family walk on eggshells, or in some other way alter their behavior, to try to avoid getting your child upset? Does your child argue, cry, or have temper tantrums much more often than other kids their age? Does your child get overexcited or become so anxious that it stops them from doing things?

BEING SELF-AWARE

Does your child seem to be oblivious to behaviors that may annoy other people or make them unhappy? Do they need to be reminded to eat when they are hungry or take a break when they are overstimulated? Do you find that they speak too loudly indoors or talk too quickly for others to understand? Do they often need special prompting to join in activities during birthday parties or other structured events?

THINKING BEFORE ACTING

Does your child engage in impulsive actions, such as grabbing things? Do they sometimes act in ways that seem to make no sense, such as knocking something over for no reason? When you ask your child why they acted this way, are they unable to answer?

STARTING TASKS

Do you find that you need to ask your child to start a task several times before they are able to get moving? Do they daydream or fidget more before starting a task, or suddenly decide that they are hungry or need a drink of water? Does your child have trouble switching from one task to another?

BEING ORGANIZED

Are your child's backpack and binders an absolute mess? Are they constantly losing simple items they need every day, such as their shoes? Are matching socks an ironic coincidence? Does their room look like a hurricane ripped through it?

THOUGHTFUL PLANNING

Does your child try to accomplish too much in one day? Do they want to finish three art projects and learn to play an instrument before tackling their homework? Do they have difficulty knowing how to prepare, such as setting out their clothes for the next day?

MANAGING TIME

Is your child always running late? Does it seem to take them forever to get dressed and out the door in the morning? Do they often still have homework to do when it is time to go to bed? Do they get lost in the shower?

DOES YOUR CHILD NEED MORE SUPPORT?

Sometimes the challenges that children face are greater than what we as parents can address alone. Professionals with expertise in executive functioning can provide consistent guidance, support, and fresh ideas. These professionals may include licensed psychologists, social workers, or mental health counselors with a specialized background in executive functioning. When you are hiring a professional, be sure to check out their background, including their education, experience, appropriate certifications or licensing, and client reviews. It is often helpful for parents to meet with the professional first to make sure they are a good match for your child before engaging their services. Finally, you may want to consider a complete medical and neuropsychological evaluation for your child to rule out anxiety, auditory processing disorders, sleep disorders, and any other medical or psychiatric issues that may impair executive functioning. Check with your pediatrician or school counselor for local resources that provide such evaluations.

THE PARENTS' TOOLBOX

Your child has a lot to learn—and one thing we know about children is that they all learn in different ways. Children engage in auditory learning by being spoken to, which is the preferred method of many parents and teachers. Children with executive functioning difficulties respond best to auditory learning that is simplified into one- or two-step commands, such as "Take your coat off" followed by "Come sit at the table." Auditory learning is also enhanced by frequent praise attached to specific behaviors; for example, "Your calendar is beautifully organized" as opposed to "You did a great job today."

But parents can go far beyond verbal teaching to enhance their child's ability to learn. For instance, children also learn visually. We can use visual cues, such as the ones found in Exercises 3, 10, 16, and 26, all around our child's environment. Visual learning also reminds us to model behaviors for our children, because they are always watching. In fact, novelist James Baldwin once said, "Children have never been very good at listening to their elders, but they have never failed to imitate them." I believe many parents will recognize this as true. One of the most difficult challenges for parents is modeling behaviors that we struggle with ourselves. After all, children inherit many of their traits from us. In these instances, we can model a growth mindset by showing our children how we are trying to grow, demonstrating persistence, taking accountability for our errors, and learning from our mistakes. We can also model asking for help, getting support, taking breaks, and self-forgiveness. These are powerful lessons our children will take with them for a lifetime.

We know that children also learn through reading and writing. Tools such as reading stories, drawing, and journaling can be beneficial. These types of tools help children slow down, observe, and evaluate their own behaviors and the behaviors of others. They also help children identify and express their emotions and to understand that they are not alone with some of the difficulties they face.

Finally, children learn through kinesthetics, or hands-on participation, too. Daily routine, practice, and repetition are essential for children to experience kinesthetic learning. When children have a routine, those routine tasks are more likely to become automatic. A daily routine, or a mini-routine such as bedtime, is a critical aspect of many areas of executive functioning (such as working memory, time management, and organization). Kinesthetic learning is also wonderful for strengthening executive functioning abilities. For instance, children can strengthen impulse control by playing any game involving taking turns. They can practice organization by grouping tasks, such as cleaning up LEGO bricks by color. Memory card games help with working memory. You can help strengthen your child's focus by baking with them and following a recipe. Many children are strong kinesthetic learners.

One of the most important aspects of learning is motivation. Children are usually eager to please and will work hard when we are taking notice of their ability to learn and succeed. As parents, we are often quick to let children know when they are engaging in an unwanted behavior, such as jumping on the furniture, but we may not think to let them know how appreciative we are when they are sitting quietly. Providing children with tons of praise and rewards for correct behaviors is called positive reinforcement, and it is a powerful learning tool.

There is no such thing as perfect parenting, but many parents feel great when they are loving, learning, and growing together along with their children. You have taken an important step in using this workbook to learn more about your child and about executive functioning, and I hope this is just one small step in a wonderful, lifelong journey.

PARENTS' TIME-OUT

Many parents are so busy with managing their children's lives that they often put themselves last. They frequently laugh at me when I stress how important self-care is, insisting there is simply no time. But parents are people, too. We need sleep, exercise, rest, grown-up fun, and support to keep thriving and doing what we need to do every day. So, please take a moment to create some ideas for your own self-care. Your list may include things like exercising, drinking water, calling a specific friend or family member, or taking a vacation. The more ideas you put on your list, the more options you will see for yourself on those days when you feel stressed out, frustrated, or tired. Post this list somewhere where it can remind you of how important you are.

Daily	Weekly	As needed

CREATE AND MAINTAIN ROUTINES

Children benefit from having a consistent, daily routine. Taking the time to plan a routine can be essential, even if it is a little different each day due to work schedules or activities. A daily routine also lets children know what to expect each day. Take a few minutes to design a daily routine for your family, and then do your best to follow it. Be as specific as you can, including things like homework time, dinnertime, bedtime, and family time. Also remember that we should always aim for improvement, not perfection.

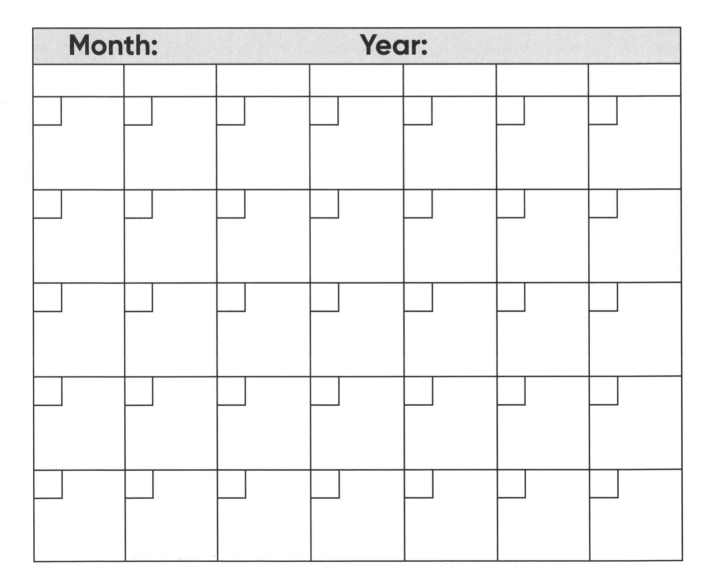

Month: **Year:**

PRAISE

There are many ways to praise your child for specific behaviors. Look at this list and identify three praise statements for you to try today. Return to this list often to remind yourself of what praise can sound like.

Thank you for helping me ....

I really like the way you ....

I'm so proud of you for ....

I love the .... that you chose to wear today.

You are so clever at ....

What a beautiful drawing. I especially like ....

I love when you ....

Wow! You really put a lot of work into ....

Great job at .... I knew you could do it!

It was so nice of you to ....

MODEL MISTAKES AND APOLOGIES

Being a parent means you are in charge, but it doesn't mean that you are perfect. All people, including parents, make mistakes or hurt someone's feelings from time to time. One of the most important takeaways from this book is a growth mindset, which means that we can acknowledge our mistakes and learn from them. Modeling appropriate apologies and expecting them from your children can be an important part of growing and learning together.

A proper apology focuses on being honest, taking responsibility, and learning from our mistakes. It goes like this:

I am sorry for ....

It was wrong because ....

Next time, I will try to ....

More Ways to Learn

Apps

Happy Kids Timer family chores app. Guides kids with animated chores and turns chores into a fun education game. Also provides an incentive program with in-game awards.

Mindful Powers app. This award-winning app allows children to use mindful play to improve focus and learn to self-regulate stress and anxiety.

Books

How Did You Miss That? A Story about Teaching Self-Monitoring by Bryan Smith. Follow Braden as he learns to slow down, be accurate, and double-check his work. (Also check out other storybooks about executive functioning by the same author!)

Mindfulness Activities for Children with ADHD: Engaging Stories and Exercises to Help You Learn and Thrive by Sharon Grand, PhD. Three adorable stories with mindfulness exercises woven throughout that help improve calm focus, self-observation, and self-regulation.

Ninja Life Hacks by Mary Nhin and Jelena Stupar. This wonderful series of books promotes a growth mindset and helps children learn valuable life skills, such as being focused, calm, and brave.

Your Kid's Gonna Be Okay: Building the Executive Functioning Skills Your Child Needs in the Age of Attention by Michael Delman, MEd. This book helps parents understand the critical skills of executive functioning and provides tools to help kids become motivated, accountable, and independent. Through engaging stories, the author demonstrates how kids can change their habits and pave a path toward improved competence.

Exercise Index

Use this exercise index to find the activities that can help improve each specific major skill.

BEING ORGANIZED

Exercises 9, 15, 16, and 28

BEING SELF-AWARE

Exercises 11, 12, 17, 18, 23, and 24

CHOOSING GOALS AND STICKING TO THEM

Exercises 3, 6, 10, and 19

COMPLETING TASKS

Exercises 26 and 38

CONTROLLING EMOTIONS

Exercises 11, 12, 17, 18, 23, and 24

MANAGING TIME

Exercises 21 and 22

STARTING TASKS

Exercises 25, 37, and 38

STAYING FOCUSED

Exercises 11, 12, 17, 18, 23, and 24

THOUGHTFUL PLANNING

Exercises 8, 13, 14, 20, 27, 30, 39, and 40

THINKING BEFORE ACTING

Exercises 11, 12, 17, 18, 23, and 24

ABOUT THE AUTHOR

Sharon Grand, PhD, BCN, is a licensed psychologist who has worked with children and families for many years. She owns Wavelengths Psychology and Neurofeedback, a private group therapy practice on Long Island, New York, and is fortunate to have an awesome team of therapists dedicated to a mind-brain-body approach to resilience and mental health. Dr. Grand loves working with children and especially loves reading books and stories together. She appreciates time spent with her son, her husband, her family, and her friends, and enjoys doing lots of things she is not very good at, including baking, singing, and dancing. Dr. Grand is personally and professionally familiar with executive functioning challenges, and uses humor and a growth mindset to keep learning and to never give up. She is proud of all the children and families who are working hard to learn and grow together, and she hopes that this book will be a wonderful part of their journey.